Dino Babies!

By Dr. Robert T. Bakker

Illustrated by Luis V. Rey

A Random House PICTUREBACK® Book

Random House 🏠 New York

The author and editor would like to thank Dr. Thomas R. Holtz, Jr., University of Maryland, for his assistance in the preparation of this book.

Text copyright © 2010 by Dr. Robert T. Bakker
Illustrations copyright © 2010 by Luis V. Rey

Visit us on the Web! www.randomhouse.com/kids

Educators and librarians, for a variety of teaching tools, visit us at
www.randomhouse.com/teachers

Library of Congress Cataloging-in-Publication Data
Bakker, Robert T.
Dino babies! / by Dr. Robert T. Bakker ; illustrated by Luis V. Rey.
p. cm. — (A Random House pictureback book)
ISBN 978-0-375-86330-1 (trade) — ISBN 978-0-375-96330-8 (lib. bdg.)
1. Dinosaurs—Infancy—Juvenile literature. I. Rey, Luis V., ill. II. Title.
QE861.5.B3438 2010   567.9—dc22   2009001283

Printed in the United States of America   10 9 8 7 6 5 4 3 2

Random House Children's Books supports the First Amendment and celebrates the right to read.

Were dinosaurs good parents?

If you were a baby *T. rex*, would your mom or dad be there to protect you? Or would you be left on your own?

What if you were a *Triceratops* (try-SEHR-uh-tops) kid, and a big meat-eater tried to grab you? Would your mom or dad rush in to save you?

There are many kinds of animal parents. A turtle mom lays her eggs in a nest, covers them with sand, then walks away. She never sees her babies again.

A crocodile mom stays close to her nest. She chases away lizards who try to steal the eggs. She protects the newly hatched crocs for up to a year.

Eagle and hawk parents work even harder. They feed their young until they're fully grown.

Were dino moms and dads like turtles? Or crocodiles?
Or eagles? Or something in between?
   I'm a paleontologist (pay-lee-uhn-TAH-luh-jist),
a scientist who studies fossils. Paleontologists study
dino families by digging up bones, teeth, eggs,
and footprints left behind in rock layers.

Fossil teeth can tell us how dino babies got their food. When dinos ate, some of their teeth would fall out, and new teeth would grow in. I found a spot in Wyoming full of baby teeth from *Allosaurus* (AL-oh-saw-rus), a meat-eater.

The babies had been eating huge chunks of plant-eating dinosaurs. How did the babies get such big hunks of meat?

From their parents! We found giant teeth from adult *Allosaurus* mixed with the baby teeth. *Allosaurus* moms and dads brought food to their young. The babies didn't have to hunt by themselves.

Today, many birds make rookeries—spots where hundreds of nests are crowded together. Did dinosaurs use rookeries?

Some did! In Argentina, we found thousands of dino eggs in hundreds of nests, all buried in mud that had turned into stone.

All the eggs came from titanosaurs (ty-TAN-oh-sawrs), long-necked plant-eaters bigger than elephants.

Dozens of the eggs had the bones of unhatched babies inside. They were no bigger than kittens.

The nests were so close together that the moms and dads had to walk very carefully so that they didn't step on the eggs. Or the babies!

Did long-necked dinosaurs take care of their kids after they left the nest? Yes! Here's how we know:

In Texas, we dug up huge fossil footprints from long-necked brachiosaurs (BRAK-ee-oh-sawrs). They were walking in a big herd. And there were small tracks too, made by youngsters hurrying to keep up with the adults.

The adult brachiosaurs were strong enough to easily crunch any predator who tried to grab a brachiosaur kid.

Not all dino moms and dads were big. Adult *Drinker*s were plant-eating dinos about the size of turkeys. I found a dozen *Drinker* skeletons, babies and adults, all crowded together in one spot in Wyoming.

What were the *Drinker*s doing there?

We x-rayed the rock. The X-ray showed that all the dinosaurs were sitting down side by side, feet flat on the ground, and facing the same direction. It was an entire dino family in their burrow! Animals use burrows as shelters from bad weather, and to hide from predators in.

Today, ostrich dads are great babysitters. They'll guard up to forty chicks at once!

Psittacosaurus (sih-TAK-oh-saw-rus) was a dinosaur babysitter. The adult was the size of a big chicken. Three dozen baby *Psittacosaurus* were found in Mongolia, all crowded around just one adult. Maybe it was Mom. Maybe it was Dad. Either way, he or she had a tough job!

Psittacosaurus ate leaves, roots, and bugs. And lots of plants and bugs are poisonous. The babies probably watched what Mom or Dad ate. That way, they learned what to eat and what to avoid.

Many plant-eating dino moms could call to their babies by blowing through tubes in their snouts. *Parasaurolophus* (PAR-uh-sawr-OH-loaf-us), found in New Mexico, had really long sound tubes.

Babies didn't have big tubes, so they just went *squeak*. But Mom could *HONK* so loud she could make the ground shake.

Moms could call to their kids from far away. *"Hey! Come back here!"* is what the call meant.

When a meat-eater attacked, a dozen *Parasaurolophus* moms might all honk at once—and give the meat-eater a splitting headache!

Adult *Triceratops* were big and dangerous. They used their long, sharp horns and massive muscles to fight *T. rex*.

But baby *Triceratops* were only as big as sheep, and their horns were slender and weak. Did their parents protect them?

Yes! Baby T'tops teeth are always found with adult T'tops teeth. If the babies were ever by themselves, we'd find just baby teeth.

A *T. rex* who tried to snatch a *Triceratops* baby might be charged by an angry mom or dad—or both! That would have been scary!

Imagine that you are a *T. rex* baby in your
nest on a dark, chilly night. What would you feel?
Your mom's warm body!

T. rex wasn't a big lizard with naked, scaly skin. Fossil skin found on tyrannosaur skeletons shows thin, hairlike feathers. That proves that rexes were hot-blooded—they had enough body heat to keep themselves and their babies warm even when it was cold outside.

Who were the very *best* dino moms and dads?
That's a tough question, but I vote for raptors!
Deinonychus (dy-NON-ih-kus) was a fast, graceful raptor the size of a wolf.
A *Deinonychus* skeleton found in Montana showed that when the dino died, it had
been sitting on its eggs. The raptor was using its arms and body to protect its

unhatched babies. Those arms had big, strong feathers! We've found many raptor skeletons preserved with skin, and all show a complete set of wide feathers, similar to a hawk's or eagle's.

Raptors had big brains. This means raptor parents were intelligent—they could play with their chicks and teach them how to hunt and outsmart enemies.

Wouldn't it be wonderful to see a live raptor? Well, we can! Modern-day birds are descendants of raptors. When you watch a mom or dad eagle feeding its babies, you are seeing a living *Deinonychus*!